# Rarest Places

Samantha Bell

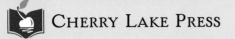
# CHERRY LAKE PRESS

Published in the United States of America by Cherry Lake Publishing Group
Ann Arbor, Michigan
www.cherrylakepublishing.com

Reading Adviser: Beth Walker Gambro, MS, Ed., Reading Consultant, Yorkville, IL

Photo Credits: cover, title page: © ocudrone/Shutterstock; page 4: © Roussein/Dreamstime.com; page 5: NPS Photo; page 7: Chris Boswell/Dreamstime.com; page 8: NPS Photo; page 11: © Francisco Blanco/Dreamstime.com; page 12: NPS Photo/Brooke Shamblin; page 13: © Francisco Blanco/Dreamstime.com; page 14: © Wilsilver77/Dreamstime.com; page 17: © John Wollwerth/Dreamstime.com; page 18: © Pierre Leclerc/Dreamstime.com; page 19: Bruce Marlin, CC BY-SA 2.5, via Wikimedia Commons; page 21: NPS Photo/Janice Wei; page 22: NPS Photo/J. Wei; page 23: rjones0856, CC BY 2.0, via Wikimedia Commons; page 24: © Helmut Watson/Dreamstime.com; page 25: NPS Photo/J.Wei; page 27: © George Burba/Dreamstime.com; page 29: NPS/Jacob Holgerson; page 30: © JlAlvarez/Shutterstock

**Cherry Lake Press** is an imprint of Cherry Lake Publishing Group.

Library of Congress Cataloging-in-Publication Data

Names: Bell, Samantha, author.
Title: Rarest places / written by Samantha Bell.
Description: Ann Arbor, Michigan : Cherry Lake Publishing, 2024. | Series: National park adventures | Audience: Grades 4-6 | Summary: "These places are like nowhere else on earth. What will you find? This title invites readers to explore the Everglades, peer into a Hawaiian volcano, and trek through the Petrified Forest in Arizona. Part of our 21st Century Skills Library, this series introduces concepts of natural sciences and social studies centered around a sense of adventure"— Provided by publisher.
Identifiers: LCCN 2023010578 | ISBN 9781668927410 (hardcover) | ISBN 9781668928462 (paperback) | ISBN 9781668929933 (ebook) | ISBN 9781668931417 (pdf)
Subjects: LCSH: National parks and reserves—United States—Juvenile literature. | Natural history—United States—Juvenile literature.
Classification: LCC E160 .B455 2024 | DDC 917.3—dc23/eng/20230327
LC record available at https://lccn.loc.gov/2023010578

Cherry Lake Publishing Group would like to acknowledge the work of the Partnership for 21st Century Learning, a Network of Battelle for Kids. Please visit http://www.battelleforkids.org/networks/p21 for more information.

Printed in the United States of America
Corporate Graphics

Note from publisher: Websites change regularly, and their future contents are outside of our control. Supervise children when conducting any recommended online searches for extended learning opportunities.

**Samantha Bell** was born and raised near Orlando, Florida. She grew up in a family of eight kids and all kinds of pets, including goats, chickens, cats, dogs, rabbits, horses, parakeets, hamsters, guinea pigs, a monkey, a raccoon, and a coatimundi. She now lives with her family in the foothills of the Blue Ridge Mountains, where she enjoys hiking, painting, and snuggling with their cats Pocket, Pebble, and Mr. Tree-Tree Triggers.

# CONTENTS

# Introduction

The United States has many unusual landscapes and **ecosystems**. The national parks help preserve these unique places. Without the parks, some of these areas may have been destroyed and lost forever. But today, people from all over the world can enjoy them. A rainforest, a river of grass, and an active volcano are just a few of the wild and wonderful places in the national parks.

# CHAPTER 1

# Hoh Rainforest

## Olympic National Park, Washington

When people think of rainforests, they often think of the tropical rainforests of the Amazon. But rainforests can be found on every continent on Earth. The Hoh Rainforest is on the western side of Olympic National Park. It sits in a deep valley surrounded by the Olympic Mountain Range. Storms develop over the Pacific Ocean. The mountains act as a funnel, bringing in rain from the storms. An average of 140 inches (356 centimeters) of rain falls in the forest each year.

The Hoh Rainforest is known as a temperate rainforest. This means the temperatures do not get very hot or cold.

Cedar trees growing in Hoh Rainforest in Olympic National Park, Washington

A hiker backpacks through Hoh Rainforest.

Temperatures in the summer usually stay below 80 degrees Fahrenheit (27 degrees C). In the winter, it rarely drops below freezing, or 32° Fahrenheit (0° C). The Hoh River flows through the rainforest. It is fed by three glaciers on Mount Olympus. It flows to the Pacific Ocean. The rainforest and the river get their name from the Hoh tribe. Today, the Hoh people live at the mouth of the river. Visitors can hike a trail that follows the river. The trail will take them many miles into the rainforest. At the end of the trail, visitors can see Mount Olympus and the Blue Glacier.

The steep mountains also protect the rainforest. They block strong winds that come in from the sea. Trees such as the Sitka spruce and western hemlock can grow and thrive. Many of the trees are hundreds of years old. Because there is so much rain, the trees grow very tall. Some reach 250 feet (76 meters) in height. Their trunks can measure up to 60 feet (18 m) around. The leaves of the trees create a lush green **canopy** at the top. Mosses and ferns cover the ground below. Roosevelt elk live in the rainforest. As they graze on the plants, they help shape the appearance of the rainforest.

# STANDING TALL

The vegetation on the ground is very dense. Because of this, seedlings do not have room to grow. Instead, many begin growing on top of fallen trees. These trees are known as nurse logs. As they grow, their roots reach to the ground. Over time, the log slowly decomposes. This provides the young trees with moisture, minerals, and warmth. When the log is gone, it looks as if the trees are standing on stilts. A row of these trees is called a **colonnade**.

# CHAPTER 2

# Sawgrass Prairie

## Everglades National Park, Florida

The Everglades is one of the largest wetlands in the world. Everglades National Park covers 2,357 square miles (6,105 square kilometers) of these wetlands. It is located on the southern tip of Florida. The park has nine different ecosystems. One is the sawgrass prairies, also called sawgrass marshes. In this ecosystem, sawgrass is the main plant. Sawgrass is not a true grass. It is a tall plant with tiny sharp ridges along the edges of each blade.

Sawgrass prairies and cypress trees in Everglades National Park, Florida

Sawgrass prairies are usually flooded with water for most of the year. Approximately 60 inches (152 cm) of rain falls during the wet season. The wet season runs from May through October. The longer the land is flooded, the taller and thicker the sawgrass grows. Fish and apple snails live underwater among the sawgrass. Alligators live in the sawgrass, too. They often make holes or depressions in the ground. From November through April, the land dries out. But many organisms continue to use the water in the alligator holes.

Alligator tracks lead to and from an alligator hole in Everglades National Park during a drought.

A sawgrass prairie by Taylor Slough
in Everglades National Park

Spanish explorers first arrived at the Everglades in 1513. At that time, the Everglades covered approximately one-third of Florida. By the mid-1800s, the United States took control of the region. But people viewed the land as useless. They tried to drain it to build homes and farms. Marjory Stoneman Douglas was a writer. She wanted to protect the Everglades. In 1947, she published a book about the area. She called the land a "river of grass" because of the slow-moving water in the sawgrass prairies. People finally began to recognize the importance of the wetlands. On December 6, 1947, the government set aside the land for Everglades National Park.

## GREAT LOSSES

When Spanish explorers arrived at the Everglades, about 20,000 members of Indigenous nations were living there. But over the years, disease and warfare left only a few hundred survivors. By 1793, many had died or moved away. Those that remained joined Indigenous groups that moved into the area later. In 1819, the United States signed a treaty with Spain that included control of Florida from Spain. They went to war against the Native Americans, forcing most of them out to Oklahoma. But some moved into the Everglades so they would not have to leave. Many of their **descendants** formed the Seminole tribe of Florida. Today, the tribe has almost 3,000 members living on six reservations. One of the reservations is in the Everglades.

# CHAPTER 3

# Bottomland Hardwood Forest

## Congaree National Park, South Carolina

During the 1800s, hundreds of trees in the South were destroyed. Many were cut down for campsites and firewood during the Civil War (1861–1865). Later, people cut down trees for lumber. In some places, the land was completely cleared. But the trees near the Congaree and Santee River systems were left alone. This forest is in a **floodplain**. The wetland made the trees difficult to harvest. Today, those trees represent the country's largest area of old-growth **bottomland hardwood forest**. Old-growth forests are trees that have developed over a long period of time. For example, a bald cypress tree

Bald cypress trees in an old-growth bottomland hardwood forest
in Congaree National Park, South Carolina

Bald cypress knees can reach more than 7 feet (2 m) high.

The forest became part of Congaree National Park. Ninety tree species grow in the forest. Besides being very old, some of the trees are also the tallest of their kind. These are known as champion trees. More champion trees are in the park than anywhere else in North America. For example, the park has the tallest sweetgum, American elm, persimmon, and laurel oak. It also has the champion loblolly pine. This pine tree rises as tall as a 17-story building. Some of the cypress trees have diameters of more than 27 feet (8 m). Part of their roots come up above the ground or water level. These roots

The trees in Congaree National Park are an important part of American history. Indigenous peoples lived in the forests long before European settlers came. They hunted the floodplain and fished in the rivers. Later, the area would serve as a place of safety for people escaping slavery. Many Black Americans stayed even after the war ended. Eventually, private landowners wanted to begin logging again. The floodplain's trees were threatened once more. Concerned citizens fought to save them, and the floodplain became a national park in 2003.

# LIGHTING UP THE NIGHT

During spring and summer, it is not unusual to see fireflies flashing their lights. But in Congaree National Park, the fireflies draw large crowds. The park is one of only a few places in the world where people can see synchronous fireflies. These fireflies all blink at the same time. They are available for viewing only for two weekends in May or June. The park must limit the number of people who come. Otherwise, the fireflies' habitat might be disrupted.

# CHAPTER 4

# Mauna Loa and Kīlauea

## Hawaii Volcanoes National Park, Hawaii

Hawaii Volcanoes National Park is located on the island of Hawaii, also known as Big Island. The park has two active volcanoes, Mauna Loa and Kīlauea. Mauna Loa is the world's largest active volcano. Its name means "long mountain" in Hawaiian. It covers half of the island. Mauna Loa rises 13,681 feet (4,170 m) above sea level. From the bottom of the sea, its height is 30,000 feet (9,144 m).

Mauna Loa and Kīlauea under a full moon in Hawaii Volcanoes National Park, Hawaii

Mauna Loa erupted for the first time in 38 years starting on November 27, 2022.

The most recent eruption on Mauna Loa was on November 27, 2022. It was the first eruption in 38 years. The volcano began spewing lava through several **fissures.** One of the fissures produced a long lava flow. It spanned more than 6 miles (10 km) in just a few days.

Kīlauea rises 4,009 feet (1,222 m) above sea level. It sits on the southeastern side of Mauna Loa. Kīlauea has been erupting almost continuously since 1983. The latest eruption began September 29, 2021. Since then, more than 29 billion gallons (109,776,941,736 liters) of lava have spewed out into the summit's crater. Many people wanted to see both volcanoes erupting at the same time. Thousands of people came to watch and take photos. But some people were nervous. They had lived through destructive eruptions.

# MORE THAN GEOLOGY

For many Native Hawaiians, volcanic eruptions have deep meaning. When Mauna Loa erupted, Hawaiians participated in traditions passed down for generations. These include dances, chants, and offerings to Pele. Pele is the beautiful Hawaiian deity of volcanoes and fire. She is said to have great power. She can cause earthquakes by stamping her feet. She starts eruptions with her anger. Through their traditions, Hawaiians honor both nature and their religion.

One way to experience the volcanoes is to hike
through the Nāhuku Lava Tube.

The full moon sets over Kīlauea at sunrise.

Visitors can experience the volcanoes in other ways. They can hike a trail around the summit of Kīlauea. Or they can hike through a rainforest to the base of a nearby crater. At the bottom is a solidified lava lake. They can hike through the Nāhuku Lava Tube. This underground passageway is 500 years old. It was created when large amounts of lava flowed underneath the surface.

# CHAPTER 5

# Petrified Forest

## Petrified Forest National Park, Arizona

The landscape in northeastern Arizona did not always look so dry. Scientists believe that it was once a vast river system. It had winding waterways and hundreds of plant species. Giant conifers rose 180 feet (55 m) into the air. Today, the area is a desert grassland. It is covered mostly by grass, as well as some desert shrubs and **succulents**. The once towering trees are now plant fossils known as petrified wood. The organic matter in the wood was replaced by natural minerals. The wood is made up of almost solid quartz. Some of the fossils are stumps. Others are complete logs. There are four large deposits of the fossils. These are called "fossil forests."

Petrified wood fossils in Petrified Forest National Park are found in many forms: stumps, pieces of logs, and complete logs.

The fossils formed because of a mineral called silica. Long ago, the logs were quickly buried by massive amounts of **sediment**. Oxygen and insects could not reach the logs. The decay of the logs slowed down. The wood had time to absorb minerals, including silica. The silica replaced the organic material. Small amounts of other minerals were also absorbed. These caused the wood to harden in different colors. The logs were very hard, but they were **brittle**. The layers of sediment caused stress on the logs. It caused them to form cracks. Over time, the cracks widened. Silica breaks at a clean angle. When the logs broke, it looked like someone had cut them.

## BREAKING THE CURSE

It is against the law to take natural items from a national park. Still, over the years, many people have taken pieces of petrified wood from the park. But there is a myth about the stolen wood. It states that the person who steals the wood will have bad luck. Many people have regretted taking the wood. They have sent it back with letters of apology. Some people sent it back for their family members, too. Park officials put the wood in a stack. They named it the "conscience pile."

The Agate House is built out of petrified wood.

The petrified wood is not the only ancient part of the park. The park also is home to more than 800 archeological and historical sites. These include a lodge called Puerco Pueblo. It was built by the Ancestral Pueblo people. It has more than 100 rooms. It was occupied between 1200 and 1400. Another building is called the Agate House. It was built from pieces of petrified wood. The Agate House was occupied from around 1100 to 1150.

# Activity

## Plan Your Adventure!

**You do not have to travel to another country to visit unique and interesting places. You can find them in the national parks! Add these rare places to your list of things to see. Then check out the other books in this series for even more ideas.**

## Getting to Know Your Neighborhood

Hemlocks, spruce, sweetgum, and oak are some of the trees that grow in the rare places mentioned in this book. You can find out what kind of trees grow in your yard or in your neighborhood. First, you will need a tree identification guide. You can find these at your library or ask an adult to help you find one online.

Next, head outside to collect some leaves. Gather a leaf or two from each tree. If you have a cell phone or a camera, take a picture of some leaves on the tree. You can use the bark and shape of the tree as clues to help you identify it.

Take each leaf and tape it to a clean sheet of paper. Look through the tree identification guide to figure out what kind of tree the leaf came from. Write the name of the tree on the paper beside the leaf.

# Learn More

## Books

Connors, Kathleen. *Petrified Forests.* New York, NY: Gareth Stevens Publishing, 2012.

McHugh, Erin. *National Parks: A Kid's Guide to America's Parks, Monuments, and Landmarks.* New York, NY: Black Dog & Leventhal Publishers, 2019.

Meinking, Mary. *What's Great About Hawaii?* Minneapolis, MN: Lerner Publications, 2016.

Nelson, Penelope. *Everglades National Park.* Minneapolis, MN: Jump, Inc!, 2020.

## On the Web

With an adult, learn more online with these suggested searches.

"Everglades Mountains and Valleys: Sawgrass Prairie." Everglades National Park.

"Hawai'i Volcanoes National Park." National Geographic Kids.

"Hoh Rain Forest." National Geographic Kids

"Petrified Forest National Park." National Geographic Kids.

# Glossary

**bottomland hardwood forest** (BAH-tuhm-land HAHRD-wuhd FOHR-uhst) a type of forest found in floodplains near large lakes and rivers

**brittle** (BRIH-tuhl) easily broken or cracked

**canopy** (KAH-nuh-pee) the top layer of branches and leaves in a rainforest

**colonnade** (kah-luh-NAYD) a series of columns

**descendants** (dih-SEN-duhnts) people who come from certain ancestors

**ecosystems** (EE-koh-sih-stuhmz) communities of living things together with their environment

**fissures** (FIH-shuhrz) narrow splits or openings in a rock

**floodplain** (FLUHD-playn) a wide, flat area of land next to a river that sometimes overflows its banks

**sediment** (SEH-duh-munt) material deposited by water, wind, or ice

**succulents** (SUH-kyoo-luhnts) plants having leaves and stems that can retain moisture, such as cacti or snake plants

**wetlands** (WET-lands) low-lying lands that are always wet

# Index